Origami Bridges

Poems of
Psychoanalysis
and Fire
. . .

Diane Ackerman

Perennial
An Imprint of HarperCollinsPublishers

First Perennial edition published 2003.

Designed by Nancy B. Field

The Library of Congress has catalogued the hardcover edition as follows:

Ackerman, Diane.
    Origami bridges: poems of psychoanalysis and fire / Diane Ackerman.—1st ed.
        p. cm.
    ISBN 0-06-019988-1
    1. Psychotherapist and patient—Poetry. 2. Psychoanalysis—Poetry.
3. Psychology—Poetry. I. Title.

PS3551.C48 O75 2002
811'.54—dc21   2002024685

ISBN 0-06-055529-7 (pbk.)

03 04 05 06 07 ❖ /RRD 10 9 8 7 6 5 4 3 2 1

Acknowledgments

. . .

Many thanks to the editors of the following periodicals where these poems first appeared.

Chelsea

"Beginning to End"

Denver Quarterly

"Those Bitches"
"Those Angels"

DoubleTake

"Matins"

First Intensity

"Christmas"
"Light at Dawn"
"Who's There?"
"Heat Wave"
"A Short Account of Longing"
"Telltale Engineering"
"On Second Thought"

Michigan Quarterly Review

"The Secret Places of Childhood"
"Luminarias"
"Imagining the Divine"

New Letters

> "The Girls"
> "Expedition"

Parnassus

> "Rorschach: Magritte's Painting 'The Therapist'"

Poetry

> "Like Your Face"
> "Report from the Sonnetarium"

Prairie Schooner

> "Cross-Country"
> "Zen Archery"
> "All Fires the Fire"
> "High Above the Impedimenta of the City"
> "The Accident"
> "Lying on the Couch"
> "Beneath the Sheets"
> "A Tournament of Fears"
> "Last Week"

Quarterly West

> "While You're Away"
> "The Shelf"

Tin House

> "The Path"
> "Watercolor by Paul Klee"
> "Blood Oranges"
> "The Unbeguiling"

Contents

. . .

The Heart's Asylum

Another Form of Midnight

Beginning to End

A Note to Readers

. . .

Perhaps readers would find it interesting to learn how these poems were written and the unusual role they played. This wasn't a planned book, but one that geysered up naturally over a year and a half, during which I wrote poems daily. I began writing them to corral the unruly emotions that arose during intense psychotherapy, a process I explain a little in this section of "Omens of Winter":

> Poems arrive as meteorites.
>
> Collecting them, I try my best to impart
> impulses, the morse code of the heart,
>
> but I do not understand the vernacular
> of fear that jostles me until art occurs,
>
> or why, know you from afar
> spurs hours of working myself into the stars.
>
> Well, I do know, but I fight its common sense:
> I try to stabilize us through eloquence.
>
> It's an old story, better told than I tell,
> how artists shape what hurts like hell
>
> (usually love) into separate empires
> of lust, tenderness, and lesser desires

An unusual aspect of my therapy was that my analyst and I lived in distant towns. Once a month or so I would visit him in his office. However, most weeks we spoke by telephone, which in some ways allowed greater intimacy and risk, although it deprived us of the lavish visual cues that can be so telling. The voice is lavish, too. I had been a telephone crisis-line counselor for several years, and so I felt comfortable dealing with steep emotions by phone, a drama which has its own fascinating dynamics. Although I don't know my doctor's background, he was a profoundly nuanced listener. Somehow this combination of methods worked remarkably well. A telephone receiver is perforated like a confessional screen, you miss the shame of eye contact, the other's voice seems to originate inside your head, mental portraits of the other form while you're talking, and so on. As in traditional psychoanalysis, you don't see the analyst. Then, when you do meet face-to-face, other elements come into play.

I sent him the poems that emerged, hot off the heart, and they became an important part of therapy, another place where we could meet. There's a tradition of using artworks in this way, children's drawings especially, and it opened up some unexpected avenues. Of course, psychotherapy and lyrical poetry address many of the same issues, and they both create a space where one can explore one's relationship with one's self and others. However, my chief goal with this book was to write the best poetry I could; its usefulness in therapy was felicitous, but secondary. That's why I sent out, and subsequently published, many of the poems in literary journals without telling the editors anything about them. They are, after all, simply deeply felt poems about one of the most important relationships in one's life.

An Alchemy
of Mind

...

LETTER TO DR. B—

I have found you among the texts
(but not the textures) of your life,
in the library of your cunning,
where the abstracts of forty papers
open, one by one, like small windows
partly sealed by terminology's lacquer.
They reveal you both aloof and enthralled,
a restless mind of intersecting planes.

How can I resist the paper "Artist and Analyst"?
Yet I do, thinking it best to stay
within the frame we've chosen,
using the palette we invent,
creating a mosaic in motion.
Whenever I set a shard in place,
the mosaic evolves, blurs a moment,
then a new scene refines, throwing past into relief,
drawing present into mind.

So I will sacrifice my yen to know
the what and whim of you. Though my curiosity
is swelling like a Magellanic Cloud
filled with a luminous starfield of questions,
I'll sacrifice them on the altar of our ineffable cause.
A padded altar. A cause quilted with passion,
and insight whose razors cut clean as thrill.
A sacrifice intoxicating as any pill.

PANDORA'S SUNDAY MORNING

You appear in darkness,
like the slowly forming crystals
of remembered thought,
eyelessly, where the brain paints
neon brush strokes
and phantoms prowl
among symbols of unrest.

While I am treading the fragile catwalk
between sleep and wakefulness,
you appear without your glasses
but in your usual chair.
I sit across from you in a floral dress.
The air trembles
with the thick smoke of emotion
as, sitting quite still,
I struggle hard towards you:
an elation like love and not like love,
a waking trance for two
powered by the interplay
of heart and mind
harnessed to work in unison.

I also sense danger alive
as the arms of a great river
closing on the soft embankments
of my life, muscling into sanity.
I have no word for this tug-of-war
whose silk rasps fiery knots
through my ribs. The verb lies somewhere
between *tempt* and *fear.*
It is not like a moaning,
but urgent as tears. I imagine
you can hear it humming in my bones.

THE ASCENT

Your building's facial muscles
set long ago in a beautiful countenance
of iron, granite, and swirling cement.
Now all who visit must pass
through a glittering darkness—
a wide cave of black stone
flashing splinters of light
with tiny patches of feldspar
translucent as skin.

I have no key to your door.
When the buzzer smarts
I respond on cue and push in,
then enter a narrow elevator
built just for two, and rise
at a surprisingly tranquil rate.

The last time I levitated
as imperceptibly as this
I was 90 feet below the waves
traveling through canyons
of brain coral and anemones,
then watching a blur
of boat and sky far above,
a guide pacing the climb,
while I surfaced in slow motion
lest my heart explode.

Oh, the bubbles that can form
in the blood, dropping one cold.
Rising, falling—in half-light
it's hard to know which way is up.
The senses are easily bedeviled.
Sometimes one needs a journeyman
to keep one's spirit level.

WHEN YOU ANSWER THE PHONE

I welcome you into the small parlor
of my ear, rearrange a few
pillows left by convention,
and settle you down in my head,
where your voice and mine
can confide at close range.

Lovers whisper like this
into one another's ears.
Parents insinuate tenderness
to their children this way,
over miles and crossed wires.

You do not lodge in my head
like an Old Testament god,
or a serial killer's deranged dog,
nor even a channeled spirit.
But you do inhabit my body
as you listen and speak,
fully present, wholly interior,
visceral, yet out of sight.

I imagine this feels a little
like lying on the couch,
beyond vision's majesty,
and letting the mind roam
until thoughts ripple
across the pond of awareness.
In truth, I would find that
too worldless to bear.

Still, without a face's expression lines
the coast is never clear.
So now and then your words travel
like a bullet between my ears.
Now and then I hear you listening,
or feel our breathing collide,

and wonder about the before
and after of our lives: the other voices,
other selves, the secret pleasures
you may indulge, all the stories left untold,
the hard quest to be known.
I lay that bundle down
each time you answer the phone.

WHEN THE SESSION ENDS

1.

The leaving feels like autumn,
a gentle, inevitable pulling back
of green thoughts, nourishment,
continuity, and light.

Just as in autumn the scarlet
always present in leaves
(but hidden beneath the potent greens
of summer) becomes visible
for the first time all year,
my insecurity shows its true color
when leaving. I fumble with thank yous.
The session ends like a small death.

2.

Yet nothing has died.
Next week we will speak again
over a wire stretched between
the tin cans of our hearts.
I will unroll the embroidery
of my dreams, and you will walk
barefoot among the delicate threads.

I will find you where I left you,
in the same mental space,
whose coordinates I am learning
by the seat of my pants—
a sort of informed roaming
flying folk name *pilotage*.

Today I add another waypoint
to the map. Every waypoint has five letters.
I will call this one "faith."

In time, will I locate
the searchlight of your regard
in fog, ice storm, or eclipse?
Will I come to trust the course
it burns through darkness,
and leave retracing that lighted path?

LYING ON THE COUCH

A wrangler in your country,
I struggle to cut truth
from life's herd of milling fibs,
try to rope and drag candor
squirming into view.
Often enough it bolts
in a mad flailing of hooves.

Truth to tell, memory lies.
Anyway, I am several,
though I correspond with all.
Which self do I address
and give unsealed to you?

The woman who wades
into deep water
holds a plank to the shore.
The woman who wisecracks
about unmade Bedouins
weeps as she nabs
a fugitive memory
in an ecstasy of shame.

Selves fly in all directions.
We net a few.
What's right for the vagabond
thwarts the homebody,
what inflames the seductress
the wounded child decries.
You touch my heart,
but can you tell me where it lies?

A TOURNAMENT OF FEARS

The fear of losing all my loved ones:
mother, father, lover.
Close in age and ailing,
they create the unstated physics
by which I live. Without it,
I would float from my gravity
boots and drift in space
beyond the orbit of light and heat.
I fear the cataclysmic day
when a small constellation
of sparkling worlds (all my points of love)
begin dwindling like dying stars.

The fear of not forgetting:
the hawks of remembrance
continue roosting on the front porch
of my memory; dwell in voices,
places; seep into any object
that does not object; force me
to handle their sharp feathers
and dine too often among carcasses.
One day only a charred skull
will remain, but even then
the hawks of remembrance
will swoop down, I fear,
and pick those bones clean.

The fear of growing old, creased by regret:
discovering the receding glaciers
of hope have left behind
the terminal morass of a life
filled with blunder, jagged peaks,
a lost kingdom of opportunities,
and, fossil perfect, the memory of love.

The fear of your knowing these fears
are only the beginning. What if my heart
starts foraging in alleys for scraps?
What if that wolf's tooth, depression,
slices my throat open, pierces my sanity,
and leaves me to drown in the magma of a mood?
What if I become a tall dark stranger?
I fear you may discover fear armors me,
and the fears I fright myself with I seek.

THE LIGHTHOUSE

I remember it was there once——
a steady blaze shining through the waves,
scattering a path of gold coins across the water,
all that bankable light:

the sun immense and inconsolable,
porridgy at its heart, annealed by fire,
scarred to within a breath of perfection:

a liquid light that construed the gloom
and gave a living, sumptuous quality,
an eminence, to everything.

I remember the great poem of matter
whose scansion filled the day with song:
a tune played on the fife of the mind,
to be sung or hummed, sacred as prayer.

But now I've wandered too far inland,
following the rich delirium of a river
to its headwaters, below canopies that shade the sky.

I've forgotten the magnitude of Canopus.
Can I see the lighthouse beacon from here?
Let me stand on your shoulders.

THE ACCIDENT

Few pains have cut deeper
than the slow-motion crack-up
with my longtime therapist
who was the respository
of my feelings, story and dreams.
The ripped metal of that bond,
littering the curb, shot sparks
with an almost gruesome beauty.

Stunned by the impact, I felt
to see if anything was broken.
Besides the badly sprained emotions
and dislocated heart, I found bleeding
rife in the sinews of the will.
Months later, I'm still limping a little.
We never meet or speak now,
and I do not imagine he thinks of me
without fearful pity.

Which is worse, I wonder,
self-blame or innocence?
If I alone caused the accident
despite my zealous swerving
then sheer madness ruled.
But suppose I didn't make it happen?
A more terrifying thought.
Then I can't make it unhappen
and I must accept how brittle,
how utterly helpless we are
despite will, wish, or reason,
always shadowed by danger
in a rampaging world.

Self-blame comes easily
when the stakes are high.
If there's nothing wrong with you,
then your loved ones fail,
if there's nothing wrong with them,
then the universe threatens.
Which is worse, I wonder,
helplessness or guilt?

UNLAWFUL ASSEMBLY

When the Secret Society
of Selves meets, it calls no one
to order, avows no creed,
follows no agenda, hangs guns
and masks at the door.
Members mingle uncomfortably,
play crazy-eights, snore.

Some are friends: clowns,
playmates, acrobats, or saints.
Others fiends. All are alone.
I hope you'll never meet them.
I wish you'd escort them home.
What unites them? I can't say.
The dues are exorbitant.
New selves never join,
nor old ones pass away.

Some are sports of nature
who creep in shadow and yearn,
and never tire of wanting
more than they deserve.
They wish you'd be their savior,
friend, lover, and muse.
But they wish not to wish you to,
and so will use any excuse
to cower in secret,
holding their bellies and whims.
But they quarrel for air
and there's never enough skin
to cover all their sores,
never enough tonic to quench
their lidless thirst.
Dare you touch their leprous hands?
The women and children first?

Some of the inner circle
are rowdy, selfish, or lewd.
You could not love them.
I do not like them.
I fear you will refuse.
You will never meet them all.
Here is the conjugation
of that desire:
You do not wish to.
I do not wish you to.
Do not wish to.
I wish you to.
Do.

BETWEEN THE CREASES

Each day I shape and fold
an origami bridge
and set it on the table
between us in space.

Only a few heartbeats wide,
it invites one to cross,
offering no escape
but views to infinity
and the illusion of falling
before one gains
entrance to the other's shore.

A strength made
from many weaknesses,
it will hold
the weight of our words
and span the furious
churnings of the river
lunging fitfully beneath.

Or lead you to a tundra
where I live in tents,
need more belongings,
but manage somehow by hand
to make origami bridges
and idols out of sand.

HIGH ABOVE
THE IMPEDIMENTA
OF THE CITY

Time falls like rain
during the hour,
soaking me in a now
and remembered present,
a deluge of long lost
yet lingering moments
so real I go beyond sweat
to a weather system
of response. My clothes drip
minutes warm as tears.

But, as I've discovered,
your office widens to contain
whole climates, even frenzied ones.
I once saw a woman leave
with blizzards spilling from her pockets,
and a man arrive in turbulence.
One patient waited
inside an aurora borealis.

I bring you my own private
Amazon, with steamy paths
to the interior, choking vines
and snake-green lusheries,
an acid sun, flute song,
piranhas and dolphins
lurking along the same banks,
rain thick as rubber,
and, at nightfall, the jungle cats of desire.
Did I mention rain?
A real toad-strangler.

What of your own weathers?
A psychosensitive office
can be driven to hysteria
by its owner's neuroses.
Then the walls start throbbing
and peeling off their paint.

Perhaps you lock away
your climate while you work.
You may swear it's only heat
howling up the registers,
but quite often, sitting on the love seat
in your waiting room,
I've heard a hurricane
prowling behind closed doors,
followed by the drum
of hail big as gazing balls.

THE RUCKUS IN MY EYES

Time and again, Svengalis captivate me.
Let's call them mentors
and say their lessons are costly.
For the sake of argument,
let's say their wizardry's spun gold
incites a welcome uprising in my soul.

Spellcraft, a wand, and certain charms
all help, but their will-crumbler
is a gaze searching as rain,
followed by supernatural care,
and insights basic as grain
that shake the foil of my curiosity
until illumination leaps.
A vague or mummified heart
adds to the mystery; then I long
to enchant the enchanter for a spell.

You're a swami running over
the hot coals of my thought.
But I'm not here to cause a ruckus
in your eyes, nor hope deep
in the filament of your bones
to embed my memory
like fuel, like fossil. I'm not here
to make you change partners
and dance, only to hymn life's fidget
and bloom, and again try
to stain the willows with a glance.

Swaying in half-light, I find myself
gripped by a steady vertigo
that begins behind my eyes
and feels like falling through snow.

THE GIRLS

I.

I only stay together
because of the children.

An eight-year-old girl
lives eternally
in a ghetto of despair
built so long ago
its crumbling walls
retain the status
of historic monument.

But for the war crimes
of one's childhood
there are no reparations.
Only the gold standard
of apology, a few coins of remorse,
and various alloys of regret.

Anyway, no one survives
to assume the blame.
Who is responsible for the deeds
of previous selves?
All the dramas happened
elsewhere, elsewhen,
to others in a distant age
of bombs, hideouts,
matinee idols and leading men.

In those lawless days
criminal acts were committed
by the innocent, one learned
unique lessons penned in blood,
the most helpless were feared most,
and the guilty could maim
with random blows of kindness.

2.

The other girl is eleven
forever and ever,
untroubled by boys,
hormones, striving, or kin.
Her freedom overflows.
The world isn't small enough
to exhaust in one lifetime.
Every day arrives
in a glittering carriage.

She may well exist
to rescue the eight-year-old
from the jaws of pain,
by distracting her
with wonder's three-ring circus,
or helping her escape
on the wings of rapture.

Because they live too far apart
—on separate time lines,
in different parallel universes—
the girls never meet.
Yet somehow they blend.

I only stay together
because of the children.

THE CONVERSATION

Why are you wading
through my stream of consciousness?
At first I could sense you
sloshing around idle reveries.
But soon you invaded
all the glades of self-communing.

Now I fight hard not to address you
when I talk to myself,
because if you become
the mind's sounding board
I'll lose my inner voice,
lose the conversation one conducts
with oneself lifelong.

When we talk out loud I'm glad
you ride my trains of thought,
absorb my absorption,
cross the narrows of a fear.
But when I'm alone,
why do you lodge in my reasoning?
How did you come to be
ghost interlocutor?

Once I unlatched the garden gate
to my facts and fancies,
you strode in and started
planting seeds, turning soil,
probing the compost of mood.
I must have led you to pools
where only my reflections had been.

But now I fight for my own echo.
I don't want you in mind
as my alter ego, receiver of alibis,
inward eye, debate judge,
perfect witness. Phantom listener,
you're too other for my pensiveness.

FILLING IN THE SPACES

You have a wife
with a pretty name
I learned glancing
at the dedication
in your new book,
while a small ingot
of jealousy fell
through my chest.

But then reason flared:
self said to self:
You want him happy,
in a well-furnished life
quilted with love.
He exists out of context
only at work—
a floating now/here world
minus past, future, yens,
quirks, sorrows, and family.

He divests himself
of self's trappings for your sake.
Bearing everything,
he bares nothing.
It's a sleight of mind.
You weave his tapestry
from the minute threads
of talk, manner, and mien.

The Acknowledgments page:
many friends, your wife again,
several gents with whom
you share a close camaraderie:
a circle richly fastened. Envy burned
a single match briefly inside.

The Introduction: when I found you
began at the beginning,
with your personality as a child,
I stopped mid-sentence
and closed the book like a handclap.

I'm not ready for your diary,
lest I fabricate what's missing;
from vellum and a few hints
create a portrait in mind-ochre,
a pigment of my imagination.

Remember Pandora?
When all the evils had flown,
the box wasn't empty.
What remained was something
crueler still: hope.
A hope that persists and kills.

RORSCHACH:
MAGRITTE'S PAINTING
"THE THERAPIST"

Behold the triangle
of moon, sack, and cane
—the months, the burdens,
the hobbling forward.

A manikin of the psyche,
he wears no visage of his own.
Yet he sits facing you
with silent candor,
legs spread like a π,
his open arms idle.

This easygoing posture
tells no age, but its poise
begs you to come close,
invites unbosoming.
One could sit for hours
on his bench-shaped lap.

Behind him a star-encrusted sky
highlights a crescent moon.
He cherishes and feels at home
among its night shadows
and ambiguous blues.
But he contains the day.

Pulled back like a theater curtain,
a voluminous old coat
reveals a fair-weather sky
tufted with clouds, a world
luminous, carefree, and remote.
His chest is a bright kingdom
one enters and then passes through.

His composure says rest,
not crippling fatigue. It's unclear
in which direction he roams.
He may be catching his breath
on a long hot pilgrimage,
or waiting at the viewer's whim.
I see him as a lone traveler,
disguised by time, who carries
the destination within him.

HARD SESSION

The roofers hammered today,
clamoring overhead as we spoke
by phone, severing the line twice,
jangling our tangled nerves.

My heart was clamoring, too,
which you heard and knew.
Dredging the past, I wasn't saying
all I felt, which you also knew.
You gave me openings,
you kept trying to break through.
I just wouldn't let you.

Afterwards, I vomited up old coins.
On one side: embarrassment.
On the other: shame. I felt bruises
the full length of our relationship.
I revealed too many debits.
My throat hurt from jagged words
like *need, want*. Everything ached.

I searched the likely places:
Had you been rejecting, fearful
or coy? Were you shamed by my shame?
Were you judging or appalled?
No, never, not at all.

The pain: a tumbler of emotion
filled to the brim; then a meniscus formed
and began spilling over. But by night
the glass was empty once more.

Now I find you where I left you
like a finely bound book I take down
from the shelf, spend time and self with,
and return to its exact place.

We haven't moved,
but I am winded from the race.

RESISTANCE

In this barefoot samba,
you mainly allow me to lead.
At times I even try to lead away
from you. Impossible.
We're engaged in tight circles,
we dash and darken together.
We swallow the music.

You know what I know
but resist knowing: I must dance
the whole dance with you,
all the dizzying moves, fever,
and ballyhoo. I stand fast,
look away, hoping against hope
that minor steps might do.

Ignore the rhythm, a voice warns;
don't chase the whirling limbs,
the flagrant eyes, the panting hips.
Song pours from my mouth.
Be a word ostrich: if you don't utter
the sounds they aren't true.

Fly, fly, the voice whispers.
But, straining at every sinew,
I only sway deeper, twirl faster.
Every pulling away draws me
closer to you, face-to-face again
as the binding dance continues.

THE LIGHTNING BOLT MAN

Time sends its nightly falcons out,
hooded, to patrol the dusk.
A tiara of stars bends
over Manhattan's skyscrapers
whose floors light up in couplets,
then stanzas of light,
whole passages I cannot read.
You know that text well,
perhaps you find its litany
a thousand words for *home*.

When we meet, I sometimes hear
low-flying planes, and marvel
how we take that for granted.
After all, time travels
only one direction in nature
and in clocks, where each moment
becomes a grander state
of disorder and everything decays—
even we who grow old
and betray our youthful dreams.
So it shouldn't surprise me
when an hour crawls or flies.
Time is the least
plausible of our fictions.

And no wonder so much remains
unsaid. For instance:
how like any bear or snake
we're both waiting in suspense
for Spring. You must sense its approach.
Doves moan from your rooftop
and pigeons strut around
your sidewalk like petitioners
at an Elizabethan court.

Ursa Major, the She-Bear
(and incidentally Artemis
or Diana, my namesake)
who guards the pole of the world,
has begun her pilgrimage.
You can tell the season
by watching her ample hips.
These days they point east at night.
That means bees will soon be
playing on small kazoos,
and self-infatuated birds
courting their reflection
in your windows. But I digress.

Sometimes I picture you
as a lightning bolt man,
tapping a twig of hard fire
on your palm, one too hot
for me to handle yet.
Translating its energy
you can singe with a touch.

Perhaps in time, I will learn
to balance that fierce heat.
But, for the moment,
it's a starry mystery.
On some level, I fathom it
as I do the coming Spring,
or the seeping of time,
or those tall paragraphs of light
you're cozy among.
I can't name or grasp it,
and yet it fills my heart with squalls
as my brain toils
for what the pulse recalls.

OMENS OF WINTER

The sun sets now in wide orange bars.
Orion is hunting among the stars

above hillsides spotted brown and white
like fawns. Poems arrive as meteorites.

Collecting them, I try my best to impart
impulses, the morse code of the heart,

but I do not understand the vernacular
of fear that jostles me until art occurs,

or why, knowing you from afar
spurs hours of working myself into the stars.

Well, I do know, but I fight its common sense:
I try to stabilize us through eloquence.

It's an old story, better told than I tell,
how artists shape what hurts like hell

(usually love) into separate empires
of lust, tenderness, and lesser desires

we can control. I barely control this one:
I wish we could feel in unison.

I wish you'd shield me from the winds of shame
that swirl up fast and sting like blame.

Some days the world feels uninhabited
and the trees look dark as arrowheads.

I wish your well-tamed inferno were mine.
My heart spanks itself. I can hear it whine.

A stranger's fire, all flash and bone,
always seems to burn brighter than our own.

PICTURE CIRCUS

You stand in the doorway
—a threshhold bridging two everywheres—
and usher me across with a smile.
At that moment I see your face
as the world does: pensive, welcoming,
able to laugh, eyes framed by spectacles
like matted prints under glass.
In dreams, we also meet for real.

But, in your office, a hotter place
for both mind and body,
I find a second face. There you suffer
a metamorphosis. Picturing
you now, I see vague features.
No personality, only a persona.

A third face: a profile.
In that low-level, undistracting,
back-of-the-mind picture circus,
you float at my right shoulder,
close, close, sometimes too close,
but always tight beside me,
light as a firefly hovering near.

I don't know why I prefer
talking face-to-face with you,
or hate to face the music,
and sometimes do an about-face.
I only know a vital facet
of facing up to you seems to require
changing your face
to keep pandemonium subdued.

RACHMANINOFF'S PSYCHIATRIST

I'm listening to Rachmaninoff's
Piano Concerto No. 2,
which he dedicated to Dr. Dahl,
the psychiatrist who guided him
through the straits of fever,
not long after Sergei had heard
his own first symphony played.
Horrified by its many defects
which seemed a sewage of noise,
he had fled the hall, ashamed,
a quagmire of self-doubt.

We cannot know all the sounds
Dahl and he exchanged,
but rubbing one word against another,
Dahl gradually restored
Sergei's confidence. History tells
that Dahl used affirmations
and auto-suggestion:
"You will compose again."
"You will write a piano concerto."
"You will write with great facility."
Repeated until the words saturated
his gift from head to fingers.

In truth, nothing can kill a gift,
but it may become anemic
from great shock or stress—
a sprain of the emotions will do,
or a traffic accident of the heart,
or a failure dire as a clanging bell.

For two years, Dahl worked
on Sergei's shattered will.
At last he collected up his senses
in a burst of blood fury

and composed his triumphant
2nd Piano Concerto,
full of tenderness and yearning,
beguiling melodies, raging passion,
and long sensuous preludes
to explosive climaxes,
frenzy followed by strains
of mysticism and trance.

Loaded with starry melodies,
it was a map of his sensibility,
and a wilderness rarely known
—the intense life of an artist
seen in miniature, with rapture expressed
as all-embracing sound.

Will you tell me if you know,
how Dahl might have received
such a gift? I cannot imagine it.
With hugs and shared enthusiasm?
With an austere thank you?
In his private moments, did he weep
at the privilege allowed him?
For a time he held the exposed heart
of a great artist, cupped his hands
around it like a flame, blew gently,
patiently, until it flared again.

For that, he earned the blessings
of history, and soothed millions
of hungry souls he would never meet.
Listening to Rachmaninoff's
concerto today, intoxicated by its fever,
I want to kiss the hands of Dahl,
but he is beyond my touch or game.
Allow me to thank you in his name.

EXPEDITION

The night feels tight as a jar
as dawn opens the lid of morning
and I dress in shadows,
struck again by the wintry lack
of birdsong, while sun lances
poke the forest floor
and small, twitchy hordes
awaken with a flinch.

Months ago, the trees revolted.
Where are the courting lizards
to do push-ups on the fence?
No exaltation of larks.
Only the clammy gray sky
torn ragged by drizzle, with clouds
textured like elephant hide.

Although we both relish
the dense jungles of the interior,
I sleep easier than you
amid the cold light of fireflies.
I miss their *femme fatale* intrigues
and golden caligraphy.

Soon I will meet you in Manhattan,
a city I love up to my tenders,
but sometimes find another form
of desert where, at night,
the sobbing of wolves
can twist deep into one's dreams.

There I will find you waiting
for us, while only blocks away,
imperceptibly, the sea will be
sloshing up and down
like a pen gliding over a chart,
and the continent reeling, too.

Where they move in concert,
a reef is formed. When *we* do,
a great barrier recedes,
the sharks of regret stop circling,
riptides loosen their grip,
and I'm no longer drowning
facedown in memories.

This pilgrimage at daybreak,
though vital now, keeps life
just uncomfortable enough
to hold addiction in check
and make finales bearable, I suspect.
But, meanwhile, I journey to you
and my own private Tibet.

The Heart's
Asylum
...

RETURNING FROM TIBET

1.

One wrong turn on a highway
as slippery as ours, and I skid
through the guardrail and plunge
over a cliff, falling like snow.
Since I'm first at the crash scene
and a doctor, I try to operate
on my wounds in the body of this poem.
Scalpel. Forceps. Clamp. Pen.

This is only exploratory verse.
With no obvious contusions,
fractures, or cuts, I hurt all over,
but in no place I can point to.
I don't know what to operate on.

2.

Maybe a fleck of memory,
sharp as a glass splinter too fine
to see, was large enough to feel.
Maybe land mines litter the mind
with hidden trip wires.
Maybe I swerved to miss hitting
a dead self in the road.
Maybe I scraped myself
paddling into the vortex of a flashback.

3.

At last I've found the node of pain,
a small point lodged deep
where attachment flows.
But the tongs of metaphor
are useless there. Extraction calls
for interplay, contact, reply.

We don't speak very often.
A week will crawl by,
and then so much depends
on a few slender minutes
which cascade like droplets
in a waterfall: slowly when you
follow one's arc and fate;
swiftly if you view them all.

4·

Yes, in dreamtime I want you
to pour into the seams of my life,
fill all the vacancies, lay down
a map of song lines. But, confess,
and I awaken the sleeping wildcat,
rejection, because you will not,
cannot comply. Your silence
takes shape as leavings inside,

while it may only be the scent
of shame and embarrassment.
Rebuff weighs more than favor
on the periodic table,
and this pain is pure unattainium,
heavy enough to send fissures
through a platinum heart.

A week ago we seemed close
as a binary star, twin lights circling
without tumbling in or away.
Today you sparkle
with the cold brilliance of rime
in another universe far off
near the beginning of time.

HOLDING RADIUM

1.

You handle me
as if composing a haiku—
a few pithy strokes
with an effect
that's pure lightning.

What does it feel like
gathering a wild, dark,
iridescent thing in your hands,
tight enough to shelter it
and even calm its trembling,
yet loose enough
not to fright or imprison it?

Sometimes how we are
is the most beautiful thing
I know—an invisible gift
I've craved since I was little.
But there's no word for it
in my heart's vocabulary.

2.

Truth is so precious
I hate parting with it.
Yet, lately, when we speak,
I open the summer house
of my sensibility to you,
and air out the private rooms
where dreams and sagas
scatter like quilts on a bed.

Still, I do not tell you
everything I imagine.

There are places I'm afraid
you may not wish to go,
say my juicy, carnal, physical
mind-play. For instance,
when you joked about
not wanting to squash a plan
of mine with your "big feet,"
I paused, before asking:
How big *are* your feet?

A tall man, you have large hands.
I wondered if all your limbs
were tall. At once I pictured you
lying naked on a summer lawn.
Succulence ensued.
All this happened in a flash,
between tock and tick.

3.

What freedom: playing with feelings
of pure experiment and risk,
knowing they'll be patrolled
by the border guards of one's will—
instead of being kidnapped
by those feelings, terrorized,
oppressed, hauled away.

I presume windswept borders
thrill you, even walking them
obliquely, without fall or mishap.
Mastering that equilibrium
must feel like holding radium.
It's a skill I long to refine,
and another new word for you
to teach me in time. Spell it slowly,
so that I can read between the lines.

HOW THE POET GOT HER STRIPES

Long ago, in the faraway land
of Midwest Childhood, there lived
a curly-haired girl who stared
through living room windows
at scenes of pure dazzlement.
Snowbanks rose shoulder-high
and she tunneled through leaf piles,
entranced by musty dustiness
as rustling colors spilled over her.

Owning a Roy Rogers writing tablet
seemed treasure abounding—
his untroubled smile, the best friend
Dale Evans lovingly beside him,
twin holsters and fringed shirts,
a glistening palomino standing ready.

She loved how pages—creamy white
with fiber flecks, and matted down
by a faint shine—smelled of new.
She loved curling letters one by one
between black lines, taking care to graze
the top line with the peak of the *a,*
drawing a belly just wide enough,
sliding a roller coaster around to the end.

No two letters matched exactly,
but she adored framing those
crafty symbols, mindful of every loop,
relishing graphite's silvery grit,
which somehow poured from a pencil
without pouring away. That small arcade
contained a fist-load of charms.

Rainy days, she watched droplets
wriggle down the windowpanes.

Standing only as tall as the tabletops,
she peered through the green ribbon
edging sheets of protective glass,
into a funhouse of twisting shapes
grown-ups didn't know about—
had she seen the ocean, she might have
recognized the waves and whales.

She hated it when her brother
taunted her or made her eat grass.
She rarely saw her father, who worked
from dawn till dinner, and anyway
didn't seem to like children very much.
He never let her touch him,
never entered the early grammar
of her life with talk or hugs.
Always there, he was always gone,
silent or yelling, full of angles.
When he wasn't looking,
she would embezzle love from him.

Mother worked at home,
in a nearby room as far away
as the sun, so the girl mainly played
on her own. *No crybabies allowed,*
mother warned, threatening,
if she cried, to leave her all alone.

In time she began devising other
kingdoms and shadow families—
thrilling treks to the Orient, spy sagas,
escape routes and asylums hidden
in plain sight—swashbuckling
fantasies where she invented a self
brave and strong and just and true,

a woman who righted wrongs,
and incited love in those she loved,
indelibly, as only children can.

For many years, her household
teemed with invisible dramas
she brewed by instinct, as basic elixir,
the way a body craves vitamins it needs.
Not a perfect tonic by a long shot,
but enough to transport her
to the dangerous world of favor,
where she mattered and thrived.

A child assumes childish things:
only heroes are lovable, pain is need,
life is magically revisable,
broken hearts don't bleed,
loving arms can be sculpted from clay,
and a better self created at speed.

Was that the source of a river
whose headwaters flow as art?
Do the poems I devise for you today
begin there, in quicksand,
with urgent flailings to breathe?

When we journey alone together
through the wild country of the soul,
and I envy your greater courage,
which looks solid as mahogany,
or your agile heart, softly flaming like pearl,
remind me of the child too small
to peer over snowbanks, who sailed
mythic seas, and handcrafted worlds.

Rinsed with sleep,
I lie abed and plumb
the newly opened vault
of childhood bullion.
The front steps: steep cement,
with black iron curlicues
where spiders lived.
The living room rug:
mouse gray, a raised design
I felt against bare skin.

The tall staircase:
shiny wooden railings
and carpeted steps
which I loved to bump down,
one by one, on my bum.

The dancing doll, Annie,
whose feet wore elastic
that slipped over my shoes.
Her hair dangled in yellow
mop strings, her long striped arms
wrapped around my neck.

The "liquid gold"
vitamins I still taste:
thick, warm, honey-orange,
dripping down my throat,
as I stood like a baby bird
with head tilted back
for mother pouring sunshine
from a teaspoon.

I couldn't reach the stove top,
but the oven door hid sweets,
the best at Christmas—

broken cookies decorated
with candy dots
dad bought at the factory.

A hot, sticky, Midwest summer.
I'm bored, I whine.
Mother wears a gypsy blouse
and splashy twirl skirt.
Straight brown hair,
pulled high into a pompadour,
falls to her shoulders
and gently curls under.
Her moist skin gleams,
young with a faint tan,
her dark eyes embrace me,
and she looks heavenly,
soft, soft, her breasts
feel so soft to nuzzle among.
She loves to cuddle me,
rock me, sit holding me
until I squirm away.

At four, that was the all
I knew: the whole world
settled between those walls.
Outside raged wild seas
where dragons surely lived.
Everything wonderful,
strong or scary loomed
out of reach, except mother
who also sat down beside me,
whose arms made a cave,
whose skirts hid well,
whose kiss healed wounds,
whose song magic soothed.

Perfect and beautiful,
she set a tiny wooden table
for tea party, and we played
Mrs. Brownie and Mrs. Smith,
gossiping about husbands
and naughty children.
Sometimes we shaped costumes
out of grocery bags—
she cut the head and armholes,
I colored with crayons.
She could make scented houses
from gingerbread and gumdrops,
or fruit hover in Jell-O.

"Were you Mrs. Brownie
or Mrs. Smith?" I ask her now
by telephone, decades later,
catching her before she dashes off
for an 18th dose of radiation.
She laughs wistfully.
A gray carpet? Yes, she says.
Do I remember the crystal chandelier?
How the mirror over the fireplace
reflected its sparkling prisms?
No, I wasn't high enough,
I remind her, but I do recall
a jungle of table legs,
"and how soft and beautiful
you looked, the prettiest,
softest thing in the world."
"That's because I was always
hugging on you," she says.
"You were the light of my life;
I used to watch you and glow."

"Do you remember all the times
you couldn't sleep, and I would sit
stroking your back for ages?"
I summon the stroking, the many nights
lying restless with a busy mind.
In such moments, a tender blur
held us fast and nothing lacked,
as mother circled her hand
round and round my flannel back,
thinking herself the luckiest
woman alive to have the girl
she'd always wanted, and how at least
this one thing turned out right.

OF A FEATHER

Abracadabra, and birds fly.
Meaty yet ghostlike, they change shape
to pirouette on high, casting daggers
of glare or broad black shadows.
To the devout, flying crucifixions.
Sitting nearly motionless on a limb,
they continue flying, but at zero speed,
as the wind soughs through them.
Even their fallen feathers fly.

Like shamans or courtiers,
they rehearse the intricate rituals
and ceremonies that rule lives.
A courting crow on the outs
performs an appeasement gesture,
dropping a succulent berry
at a glossy female's feet.
She stops chattering abuse,
edges closer, burbles, rolls a rebus eye.
Another male stages his own
private one-bird vaudeville show,
with hopscotch, tap dance,
acrobatics, trendy tunes.

Aloft, birds look like parts of sky
that have broken loose.
Alternately angelic and stark,
they slide across the blue on wings
softer than skin, soft as our gold standard
for softness, while constantly
opening and closing an array
of small doors in their wings
(closed with each downflap,
for cupping the air, then open on upflaps
so air can stream through). Masters

of silent commotion, do they hear,
feel door feathers slamming shut?

In wistfulness and envy, I gaze at them,
lamenting just how earthbound I live,
and sigh the poignant subjunctive
of our species: *If only.* If only
I could beguile the winds, if only
I could float the sky upon my shoulders.

THE PATH

When the fog begins lifting
I discover a path
winding down the jagged cliff,
past abandoned mine shafts
along a trail fluorescent
with Tibetan moss and prayers,
across the high plateaux
where ice cascades in opal tusks,
beyond a grassy hillside's flanks,
through lowland swamps,
all the way back to contractions
of light on the horizon —
a trail only visible in reverse,
a map in hindsight.

Even at a distance I can spot,
jutting out from crevices,
fields of wildflowers I've kept for years
without recalling their origin,
can see ravines where palm-sized rocks
I've worn smooth from handling —
ones engraved with WONDER
and CARPE DIEM — were quarried.

Upturning my knapsack,
I pour its assortment of plants,
rocks, fossils, and curiosities
on the ground, identifying each
and where it was gathered,
study photographs of waypoints
shared with bygone friends.
Arranging them in a small altar
by the roadside lightens my load.
Then I hoist my pack, turn again
toward a gold crest floating
above the timberline, and check the route:
my compass points forward.

THE MOLLY GIRL

Who they were, how they looked—
memories flit like dragonflies
as, one by one, her childhood
friends spiral in and die.

Because they knew her as a girl,
she feels her youth die with them, too,
and panics as the crowd thins
between oblivion and her.

Once a skinny teen named Molly,
with lanky brown hair;
she's zaftig now, renamed Marcia,
a curly blond octogenarian.

But the Molly girl,
how can the Molly girl die,
when she still feels like that chorister
of coquettish sighs?

I cannot curb her fright
as she loses childhood friends,
cannot know the Molly girl
though I've met her now and then.

As long as those pals lasted
she lived young in their mind's eye.
They furnished her childhood.
How can a Molly die?

I can't revive Molly's utopia,
can't unbend time's curvature,
but I believe there lived and loved once
a frisky scamp like her.

CLOUDS AND VASES

Memory's accomplice,
words carve only small shapes
in the formless clamor
of the world, yet they *are* shapes—
bright vessels I can arrange,
scrub, and refill.

Defined by their limits,
they're all edge and outline
with brittle insides.
But turned on the wheel
of a spinning mood,
they harden into *felt,*
become stiff enough
to hold untidy emotions
for a while, even steady
a fiery cargo (like love)
with abiding graces.

As you may have gathered,
I collect vases.

You collect clouds.

When we speak, breath and heart
stream together,
as we enter into the spirit
of each other, mixing our elements
in an alchemy of mind.
Clouds mingle easily,
though they're less tangible and exact.
Nebulous feelings can surge
into a stratosphere of woe,
but they also rise to heights
mere words can't go:

the land of pain's nimbus
and the loon's adagio.

The vase I'm clutching now
is a timepool, sleek as bone,
bright vermillion, abounding
with boundaries, of course,
and tense enough to balance
most impulses or yens.
I will not fill it with tears
or roses until we speak again.

LUMINARIAS

I

The hilltop pond reflects
a fierce rootedness of tall grass
and resiliency of wildflowers,
but also the dome of the sky
filled with the inexhaustible
parade of clouds and birds.

At night, it serves
the tumbling well of space,
a greater darkness between the reeds
where moonlight skitters
in a wilderness of stars.

Bags of fire line a path
spiraling through the hospice gardens
where we stroll
remembering someone
who lived like a torch,
or had a magic lantern heart,
or powered a lighthouse.

We, too, are bags of fire
wearing a thin papery shield
between us and the weathers.
We burn like tallow, we taper off,
a candle in every cell.

At night in the ocean
lights turn on like kitchen bulbs,
as animals kindle a glow
to read by—at staggering depths
they don't need eyes
to fathom the darkness.

We do, as we travel
the shoals of memory
and drift between flickering
live fire and shadow,
for we belong to our past,
whose mooring lines sway
invisibly when we move.
But we also belong to our time.
Both hold starry inlets
and waypoints,
from childhood's embers
to love's meteoric sighs,
as we follow our flare path
between the earth and sky.

II

Dark pathways wound several knots
among themselves. The trail vanished
as night fell, and clarinets played a fugue
of notes, body pulse and brain-beat,
pouring song down shiny spigots.
As a silver dollar moon floated
in the well of space, a minister celebrated
the departed with images of light.

The pond reflected stars, then inked down,
and trembled like the carapace of a beetle,
before it threw open sparkling windows
to another world. Fire-rafts floated as taps played,
and a hundred or so folk made pilgrimage
to the water's edge, where the tall grass
of reason leads to flat, calm insensibility.

Meanwhile, the bagged infernos blazed.
Imagine: capturing flame in paper.

That would have astonished our ancestors.
Such an ordinary miracle we construe
as beauty tonight, and a shared symbol
of loss felt privately in public,
because like the ancients, we're still driven
to perform our ceremonies of grief
with fire, earth, water, and elemental love.

III

I can see you now, settled in a chair
as you picture this night scene,
beguiled by stars showering glitter
onto the water, touched by the sundry ports
of light—each a small memory pyre—
can see your backbone's long row of luminarias
fed by kinship and a holy fire.

CROSS-COUNTRY

Sun, snow, glitter-wings.
I glide *shush, shush* on a crusty day.
Memory's angels cut figures in glare:
tiny ones like paper dolls;
naked snow angels on a dare
with a lover years later.

A sign posted on the golf course
at the wood's edge:
  PLAY FAST
  DON'T LET SPACE
  OPEN AHEAD OF YOU
I try to oblige, wind to my back,
ski-sailing, brisk as a clipper ship.

The cradle glide of skiing
feels langorous, swaysome, slick.
I am a metal slide on an autoharp.
Country music plays: songbirds
returning from winter digs,
ice crackle, twig fall, honking geese,
wind snarls, howling baboonery.

Swooping downhill
through brush, riding ski edges,
while pole pendulums balance
high-wire arms, and the world
films by, I borrow ruts forged
by another skier and zoom
turbo-charged, as I fling snow roosters
and zing along, gouging hoofmarks
with the poles, until I bottom out
and glide again through
the next field of loopholes.

Like riverbanks or breaths,
ski tracks come in pairs.
These parallel thoughts slide
with me, too, alternating lead:
the air pure as a mantra
below a snazzy blue sky,
and you, strangely alongside,
chattable, pocketed with care,
but outside my senses.

I'm glad you do not answer
in a dialect of windspeak:
drum roll, sips, tribal ululation,
owl call, banshee moan.
Scented by iced buds,
the air tastes ripe and tinny,
but does not include you
in essence, though I wish
you could savor it, too.
Shall I spread it
on bread and send it?

Back to the snowflakes
falling like shredded wax
and the wind flexing its muscles
over skiddy terrain. These days
I sometimes glide around you,
or with you side-by-side, breathless,
but taking either in stride.

STUBBS'S HONEYMOON

On his honeymoon, 18th-century painter
George Stubbs insisted that he and his new
wife share their cottage with a half-dissected
horse he was painting.

Plunge your hands in the wounds.
Do not shake off the blood or flints
of shattered bone. Feel the wild shambles
that transport me. I draw its liveliness
like water from the well of death.

Here you see the chaos that fires
each muscle, and how from lather and toil,
with lashings at the bone, a mere beast
becomes the elegant lines you ride
tenderly, admiring its grace-sprung power.

Here you see the churning humors
beneath the mask of ice, a horse no longer
fleet but clumsy, a dangling fool
of guts and hide. Can you love it now
without the polish and upholstery?

Do you still find it beautiful?
I must know for certain. Grope beyond the ribs
for the red blossom of the heart.
Here, let me show you. Press it to your lips.
Do not be afraid, come closer.

THE UNBEGUILING

When we summit in Tibet,
I try to keep the abominable
in its den: *La bête,*
who famishes and repents
and worships only roses.

Prey to unrequited love,
he is a *ménage à un.*
Perhaps he's not as pitiable
as I suppose. But suppose he is

a sniveling monstrosity
who's hostile and melancholy
and frankly a need-pit,
purity's venegance, a gaping gut?

What's worse, other mutants
squint from their caves—
the marauder, the moron,
the miser, the jackal, the slut,
the small Napoleon. All bona fide.

I jest about them, but fear
they'll slip their leashes
in an unearthly uproar
and pose in tents along the midway
where you'll be repelled,
and I'll discover that
I can't unring hell's bells.

A LITTLE GRAMMAR IS
A DANGEROUS THING

Once life was all verbs—
discover, marvel, write, love, dare.

You inhabit a land of pronouns—
I, you, him, her, us, my, their.

Together we visit the past perfect's
gentry—all the haves and have-nots;
endure the agitated conditional—
what if, could have been, if only, otherwise.

But the intense mood is where
I really specialize—
Do I employ or implore you?
And also the first-person transcendental—
Would that my spirit took wing.

A word-slut, I'll tense anything
that dangles or can be modified,
spinning dreams of a future perfect,
until I suffer delusions of candor
and become a misplaced aberrant.

An idea in aspic is a word.

We could dissect that image
over lunch, were it not for a cardinal
rule of analytical grammar:
never end a sentence with a proposition.

So you'll have to trust
that at the diner around the corner,
where the catch of the day is flu
and a poetic young waitress
rhymes her bell-like hips as she walks,
I've ordered you a caffe latte
and a double entendre to go.

ON SECOND THOUGHT

No, I don't read auras.
But I smell rain on umbrellas
and imagine where it fell.

I stand where deer browsed
and inhale the hot heavy musk
they leave as calling cards.

I wrap us in the sheets
of a freshly starched enigma.
(Time loves a mystery.)

No, I don't sense auras.
But I believe in spirit guides
like you, sleights of mind,

being whammied, the soul's progress,
the guarantee of wishbones,
reading the past's entrails,

powerful incantations,
love's sorcery, and even
the numerology of our regard.

Some days I'm pure ectoplasm.
Others I'm so grounded
I can see waterlilies grow,

or detect a sliver of worry
in your voice about something
that doesn't involve me,

though I pain to think
it's whittling your mood.
On second thought,
maybe I do read auras.

WE'LL ALWAYS HAVE TIBET

You're tall for a sherpa
but that's the wonder
of this boomtown amid the clouds
whose pinnacles stab
the jet stream and the stalls
of heaven, a land bordered
by time, where clocks resound
like temple bells
and begging bowls fill
when one isn't looking,
a land far from the churnings
of daily butter,
and sacred as the room
where lovers sojourn
on stolen afternoons,
a land lost in snow scarves.

Others may read or visit
its dramas, arriving flushed
from the climb and exhilarated
by the view, to drink from its wells,
as I do, but they can't reach
the Inner City where we meet,
trade, feast, and also fast,
where the streets are washed by tears,
and a bird flies with each laugh.
That hidden world
will always ever be ours apart,
its gates sprung by passwords
we've come to know by heart.

TELLTALE ENGINEERING

Wearing love's tourniquet
I entered your ward
with severed thoughts.

Soon I became a gentle solicitor
trying my case
in the court of appeals.

Then baring the archaeology
of my need, I spoke to you
in a dialect of bones.

Now you drive me
to the azimuth of desire
in my dreams.

And next?
What unfailing bridge
will I create to span
the invisible between us?

Will it involve planks
of memory? A trial balloon?
A causeway of men?
Hope's slippery pontoons?

It's hard to spot the invisible.
Even harder to tell when it's not there.
Hence all the risky dramas
and sometimes the amens.

History doesn't teach us
not to repeat mistaken identities,
only to notice
when we devise them again.

THE SOON AND DISTANT PAST

A rule of nature is that poisons
and their antidotes grow side by side.
Hence our forays to lost worlds
beyond the suburbs of thought.
We journey there as allies
piercing enemy lines, alert for land mines,
fresh hostilities or ambush.
The last few yards I crawl alone.

When I arrive, gunfire starts.
I materialize. The exit vanishes.
I cannot float above the scene
like a ghost. I am not out of my body.
No calluses armor my will.
Pouring straight down my spine,
I come to my senses in anguish.
Even my fingerprints ache.
After a brief while, I burn to escape.

Perhaps one day I will map
a shortcut back, or your arms
will plunge through like a ladder.
I'm sorry I keep apologizing
for my disarray. I know the past
wasn't rebuilt in a year, but worry
the bridge may fall as torrents rage
and I'll be lost, time's castaway.

THE HAUNTING

(spring solstice)

Going toward the light
the sun slides
the moon fiddles
and resin fills the sky.

Myrtle trees play
the green accordion of their leaves,
cats bray and claw time
to a halt.

One woman taps a tune
thunka-thack-thunk
on clothespins.

Two women sing
into a gourd
they cup like a chalice.

A blue dress sashays
around the room,
girls dance together
in an oompa-pa-pa rhythm.

A man slices open his violin
with sound.

The outline of a beast-woman
stands in the shadows:
a wolf at the door.

The moon tugs at my sleeve
and I worry, will I tumble,
will the small gully in my mood
widen to a crater?

What if my favorite haunts
fill with ghosts again?

Moving in firelight,
I'm shadowed by a phantom
whose talons
I've evaded for months.

Later in a prosperity ritual
we burn paper wishes
and whole magnolia leaves
whose sparks turn into fireflies.

On my wish-paper I write
a caution once received
in a fortune cookie:
"Do not give your heart
to the grim silent one."

IN MY DREAM
NOTHING SUPERNATURAL
HAPPENS

Fringed in tassels,
a blue hammock
lolls like a burnoose
from exposed porch beams
where it cocoons us,
blending our mouths
with sticky kisses.

Wrapped tight as a single ear
of maize, we bake in the sun,
basted by sighs.
My spine is a rosary
you know bead by bead.

Your key fits my lock
and the door of my flesh
opens wide for you
in another, more honeyed
way of knowing.

Like two bat wings
my dark eyes beat
as new hungers dizzy us
and spot welds arc
to the core of us.

Love heightens our senses,
but also limits them:
a tender blur holds us fast,
the outer world flattens
and we remap it, exploring
new trade routes to the interior.

There we find ourselves
in mirrored alleyways
lining each port of call,
among reflections
timeless and complete.
When we make love
nothing supernatural
happens, only us
and minor miracles of light.

THE WORK OF THE POET
IS TO NAME WHAT IS HOLY

The work of the poet
is to name what is holy:

the spring snow
that hides unevenness
but also records
a dog walked at lunchtime,
the hieroglyphs of birds,
pawprints of a life
tiny but resolute;

how, like Russian dolls,
we nest in previous selves;

the lustrous itch
that compels an oyster
to forge a pearl,
or a poet a verse;

the drawing on of evening
belted at the waist;

snowfields of diamond dust;

the cozy monotony
of our days, in which
love appears with a holler;

the way a man's body
has its own geography—
cliffs, aqueducts, pumice fields,
but a woman's is the jungle,
hot, steamy, full of song;

the brain's curiosity shop
filled with quaint mementos
and shadowy antiques
hidden away in drawers;

the plain geometry
of you, me, and art—
our angles at rest
among shifting forms.

The work of the poet
is to name what is holy,

and not to mind so much
the pinch of words
to cope with memories
weak as falling buildings,

or render loss, love,
and the penitentiary
of worry where we live.

The work of the poet
is to name what is holy,
a task fit for eternity,
or the small Eden of this hour.

AT THE EDGE OF THE KNOWN

We distill truth in a jungle
clearing where you learn
the native hearsay of my life
whose myths and legends
reveal my tribe's past, fetishes,
kinship and taboos.

The big picture: as a nuanced listener
and ecologist of the psyche,
you do see the forest for the trees,

but not many of my quirky tastes,
only a scattering of oases
where my curiosity dines,
just a peek at the closet meditations
where I store my moods,
rarely a health update, precious
few of my raving passions.

Did you know I've painted
my study the color
of spring light in the forest?

Or that *floaters* in my eyes
often plague me
with a small meteor storm?

In these cropped hours,
though our hearts devour them,
what can be known
of a life and the assemblage
it grows to embrace?
Hardly anything but the shadow
of a fragment of a trace.

Another Form
of Midnight
...

WEATHERING DEPRESSION

Out in the game fields
where grain once flourished
a dark cone
whipped up a frenzy:
brute force sucking madness
through stagnant wind.

Shutters ripped off nails
and cartwheel-clattered
down the street, then porches
tore straight away,
thwacking and rumbling,
while I huddled in my cellar
and held tighter, tighter,
as, outside, winds screamed
and inside shattered glass
scattered like rice.

The destruction followed
a precise, narrow path
of maximum loss
between the townships
of January and October.
On either side
cows continued grazing,
children kept jawing
in schoolyards,
newspapers were delivered,
and time's lottery chose
another million souls.

No one dodges a cyclone.
One just hopes to end up
vertical on level ground,
with nourishment of sorts,
strong knees and relief maps,
the stamina to rebuild,
and something left to pawn.

ON OTHER COUCHES

Hammock land
they call the odd shock of forest
springing up in the middle
of an open field: first one tree
takes root, swaying like a hammock,
then small animals come to rest,
bringing seeds and leavings.

The sky curdles at 4 P.M. each day,
as blue scarves trail down
from soggy clouds,
sea-oat heads blast apart,
cascading upward,
and the pursuing rain sounds
like falling butterscotch.

A typhoon of swallows
funnels into one myrtle tree,
eats the luscious berries,
and swirls away.

Salamanders travel the raised boardwalk
as small silent jeeps.

In stilted cottages
connected by raised walkways,
artists live like a troupe of wild macaques
nestled in the green bosoms
of the trees, high above
a thick, dense forest floor
leprosy-prone armadillos
share with wild pigs, raccoons,
foxes and pine snakes.

Lying on a rattan sofa,
I am beside myself
in one of the cottages,
below fans twirling slowly
like idling propellers,
as I consider the sprawl
of my life: pinnacles, swamps,
secret glades, deadend trails.

Reflecting at the window,
I see a pair of thinly clad lovers
with vertebrae clear as dice,
necking far from the resort
of home and family, gambling
everything on stolen days
in this floating green casino.
Committing love like madmen,
they are the bravest things
in a sea of blooming uproar.

The long Lucite rods
that open and close Venetian blinds
hurl prisms of sunlight
at pale walls. Who can split
the white light of a mood
so precisely?

Although my heart has traveled
many of love's countries,
the state of happiness
has some bylaws I've yet to learn.
Knowing this, I drift asleep
under a raw-beamed ceiling
where wood tangles with itself
in small private knots.

THE FATIGUE

My mind drags, idle specimen,
after a week's hard labor
of travel, students, workmen,
sleepless heart-quavers,
petty decisions and indecisions,
and a hundred time shavers.

I feel disorganized as a sneeze.
Fatigue carries the child
heavily in its arms, unbeguiled,
craving a magic remedy—
can't you reach in, shaman wild,
and extract the malady?

Weary, weary. The father pain
weighs heavy as a crushing rain.
I wish I could banish its old refrain.
Can't I just give it all to you
to haul beyond a psychic Timbuktu?
Sure you can, I hear. *Do.*

But how? Scream? Until my lungs ache?
For a week of wishdays? If I raged
like a gong, would the repercussions
slay me? Would my skin explode
with a thundercrack of bones
and sanity shatter if I expressed

the raw of it, I mean like *expressing*
juice from an orange by pressing
its soft ribs across a metal sieve.
Anyway, I don't know what the *it* is.
How do I make it physical enough
to spit up like a toad of disgust?

How shall I paint ghosts?
Well-behaved, ashamed, I boil
with the lid on tight, recoil
from accepting you in father pose,
disappoint you, I suppose,
fall short of what's uppermost.

Oh, why bother to give all again,
open the angle of one's heart again,
haggle in the grand bazaar again,
risk the camels of one's pride again,
fend again, try to mend again,
spin wheels in sand again?

I ravel and unravel.
Nothing lasts. Not hope. Not love.
Not gems held in the glove
of the mind. Stop trying. Stop caring.
Stop crying. Stop baring.
Wilt, hollow-eyed. Learn to fast.

Have you noticed shadows
are really blue? Evening is shadow.
And this sagging mood. Even the moon
needs smelling salts tonight. A window
yawns opens. Maybe if I sing to you
darkness will escape like fumes.

BLOOD ORANGES

Crescent bruises of red-purple
like carp twitching at sunset,
the slices explode in my mouth,
gushing wet, berry-fleshed.
When they are gone, I crave more
but feel lucky, not lacking.

Tower bells ring tenor and bass
across campus, their melody
gold-leaf tumbled by sun.
When silence reigns again,
I don't construe the lull
as forever or a personal defeat.

Lifting my bouquet from its vase,
I hand it to you, and you inhale
art's secretions, desire's cargo,
the volatile scent of my dreams.
I pour from the pitcher of my senses.
Stranger, I know you're thirsty;
pause a while and drink.

Whenever our eyes strike like flints
a small flame of knowing
warms the hollow of my spine.
Later, sometimes, I discover
how absence unfolds into loss,
its second nature, and a lead sinker
tugs my heart down.

It's then I wish I could embrace
love's skeleton, without foreboding,
learn to bless the insolent purity
of all communions tart and sweet,
luminous by design, perfectly deformed,
and improbable as blood oranges.

CONFIDENCE GAMES

Your book flirts with me.
Offering the mind-quest
I relish, it creeps closer
to the edge of the shelf,
making room for me
to slip between its covers.
Shall I stow it in my carry-on
and gamble with our world
at 35,000 feet
above the tawny flush
of Kansas wheat?

I resist, unready. Not unready
lest I glimpse you opening up
tight folds, like reverse origami,
to bare intersecting planes of concern,
belief orchards bordered
by the hedgerows of consequence,
and several bladelike creases
left from measuring the exact
latitude and longitude of desire.

Not unready for the public face
drawn by living out loud,
a semiformal portrait that evolves
into an iconography of self,
despite the life-freckled bones
and picturesque viscera beneath.

Not as a moth feels unready
for the singeing flame.

No, gentle wolf of insight,
it's that knowing your fascinations
I might unwittingly echo them,
and flimflam myself in the end,
trading my fitting fleece
for love's hide once again.

MISCHIEF MINDS ITS MANNERS
WHEN WE SPEAK

Mischief minds its manners when we speak.
I don't picture you bubbling with laughter,
coming unglued, getting under my skin.
(Except *now* I do in spades, in stalagtites.)
But when we speak, I bridle the ample mare
of my sensuality, ignore her steamy flanks
heating my legs, her rapid breath that creates
clouds on frosty mornings. I don't dampen
from the weather system she sometimes stirs
in my limbs, nor describe the lusty galloping,
the heat, the blur of mixing hooves and heartbeats.
Mischief minds its manners when we speak.

ZEN ARCHERY

"The hitter and hit are no longer
two opposite objects, but are one reality."
—Zen in the Art of Archery

From your quiver,
you pull the right arrow
for a long shot
over the sordid and restless.

The bow of thought bends,
and a string of words releases
insight's arrow,
which doesn't fly
straightaway to the target.

Our best work happens
when we aim at ourselves,
not speculate about
but experience each other,
get lost together.

Talk is the pretext.
I struggle not to struggle
as you grasp my mind,
guiding it slowly to the unfamiliar
feel of certain notions.

To reach this dynamic calm
the brain needs something
solid to hold. I concentrate on us.
Heavy words lead to lightness,
as we slide right over events,
objects, and other ways of being
where thought tends to stick.

In vibrant moments, we vibrate together,
immersed, unencumbered.
Perfect a frame and it frees.
Only great strength
could make it seem so effortless
to unpuzzle the heart, untrain the eye,
draw a slow string of breaths,
become the aim, let fly.

THE ORIGINS OF DESIRE

After the first axe of love,
the royal palaces splinter
as the Atlantis of childhood
sinks below memory waves,
laughter drowns,
and truth dissolves in tear-salt.

What ruins remain?
Scattered fragments of mosaic
—a shove here, a cry there,
nubby fabric, dark pain,
cameo debris potent as myth.
Too saturated to fade, they refuse
the metamorphosis of symbol.

If only they *were* symbols,
those bright tiles of sensation,
hard as rubble, jagged shards
of an event the brain snags on,
fidgets with like a holy relic
without remembering why.

Muscle memory, dancers call it.
Because the heart is muscle,
the dance continues
without plan, sense or season.

Meanwhile, on the harp of the mind,
ritual fingers pluck
at phrases of an ancient song
the body remembers,
the senses remember,
even the feelings remember.
The mind alone forgets.

SKIRTS AND BANGS

Sometimes I slip behind my bangs
where I'm child enough to believe
I can hide in plain sight
below a hem of curls, in my private Illinois
of days shorter than waist high,
when I run to mother out on the lawn
dad used to cut with a push mower
whose chattering blades
once diced up a garter snake,
run from something dark in my life
to mother, a tree I can hide behind,

and roll tight in her cotton skirt,
lightly starched, cool against my skin,
closing my eyelids to disappear
the world, as I huddle in soft fabric
and perfume, almost like crawling back
inside, unborn, once again her
little hobo clutching rib rails,
her tiny madman in a padded cell.

Hand idling on my shoulder
she awkwardly tells a neighbor:
Shy, she's just shy, then cajoles:
Come out now, Diane, come on out!
and I can feel them staring at me,
talking at me, their puzzled faces,
mother flustered. (I'm acting weird,
not shy-flirty like other children,
but mummified.) *Oh, she's just shy,*
their voices fussing me, until at last,
I peek out, laughing, pretending
it's only a game, joking to hide the hiding
but always her little stranger,
the lark's egg left in the robin's nest.

Sinking back behind my bangs
becoming small as the world felt,
I still wish I could run across the lawn
to where mother waits, and hide
far from lightning buzz, choking heat,
and a fierce Midwestern need,
under cotton wings and scented veils,
inhaling mother's calm, safe
in the garment district of her love.

A SHORT ACCOUNT OF LONGING

Give a man enough rope
and he'll wrap himself
around your little finger.

A joke, sometimes true.
(That's why women
wear a crumpled smile
between their legs.)

Too bad the rope trick
doesn't work with you.
As vacation looms
and I sense you slipping
into the provinces of your life,
my hand opens and closes
on air, and I freeze—
a deer startled by headlights.

Sometimes I forget feelings
aren't the body's main business,
only spillage created
by adaptative yens seeping
through the shale of evolution.

I forget how, like mules,
they carry up treacherous paths,
but are stubborn,
and tend to fight back.

Today, for instance,
I'm a mood wearing a dress,
trying to compose myself
in words, indisposed in stanzas.

Poems have become
a safe house where we meet
and you sometimes find
the manuscript of our endeavors
illuminated by mind light.

Or, paper bridges, they reach
between felt and spoken,
a gulf freight must cross
to reach the trade routes of said.

Among the cargo is passion
gift-wrapped in words.
Bon bons and bon mots.
Of late, we sample them
less often, and I miss
their secret tidings and gripes.

Wittgenstein quipped:
"What can't be said can't be said
and can't be whistled either."
Yet one can hear all
the vowels of the wind,
a short account of longing,
as they whistle through
the veils of a poem.

Suppose, armed and dangerous,
swinging the nightstick
of desire, you used words
as edged weapons? Others have.
I do not think you will.
But meanwhile, I'm forging
and polishing poems
I hope will ring like glaring steel.

ROCK LIONS

A figment leaps into view,
camouflaged and brawny.
Only seated in *your* chair
can I spot the lions
hidden in the outcrop
beneath a side table.

Jung might have called them
psychic knots. Lions are cozier
denizens of the mind.
Don't forget their pride.
Or how the brutal, when tamed,
still can petrify.

Another lion, sketched
and framed, lounges on the wall,
cuddly, smoochable,
with the slack mouth of a man
who once smoked a pipe.
The rock lions are different,
more dreamlike and lawless,
a haunting in stone.

Oh, to sit alone
among beautiful beasts
that can rip your heart out,
and not always be listening
for the scratch of claws on rock,
to be prey to the invisible
and indivisible, transfixed
by that embedded roar.

MEN LEAVE

As fog lifts
off the rose garden
like a comforter
gliding over blooms,
clinging at the thorns,
I watch dawn stretch
yellow arms
around the forest.

Ruby, the hummingbird,
zigzags to the feeder
as he does at 6:30
every morning,
and together we drink
the nectar of being.

Then I miss you
like a hard punch
in the stomach.

The kids are restless,
sensing you leaving.
Who will hear?
Who will watch them
ghosting around
my bone-house?

They don't believe
you will return, ever.
Men leave.
They hum the leaving song
and shut their eyes
as they bundle close
together in their arms.

In time, they'll hide
and seek again,
mind their manners,
sometimes,
forget the missing
word, sometimes.

But this morning,
though sun mice
are nosing around
the tree trunks,
and gray squirrels
in white aprons
are daring them to play,
the kids are sitting
in corners and rocking,
humming the melody
men leave.

HEAT WAVE

This torrid summer is a waste of rain.
Even the roads are melting, bleeding tar.
But for icicles under the heart,
I swear I'd overheat again.
Somewhere around the bend
you're starring in your own life.
In mine, I rearrange the sky.

Butter-and-eggs dot the roadway,
loosestrife thrives in the fields,
prickly thistle flowers
anguish in blue, and selves clamor
to be fed, as they always do.

My sweat steams as it hits
the crossbar's metal.
It's too hot to swim, let alone cycle.
But there's a myth of cool
in rushing air, so I pedal fast
until I run out of gears, then coast
toward a mirage of water.

In September it might not be cold.
Still, rime tends to form
on the windows of the soul,
and the silent auction of the flesh
is always cause for despair.
I wonder how I'll return to you:
Ensnared? Keeping the heart's dare?
Simply, without fanfare?
The only time I hate you
is when you make me care.

THE GARDEN GHOST

Sunlight pricks a spot
on the leaf floor
and blasts it into focus.
Red lichen has left bloodstains
on chewy-barked trees.
A thick blanket of leaves
gives every motion away:
falling berry, scuffling vole,
hipless garter snake.
Trees rustle like rain
as bees saw through the air,
frogs plunk at banjo strings,
and a choir of cicadas
wing-screeches in unison.

At the far rim of hearing,
from inside the house,
the answering machine speaks
with achieved casualness—
my voice tells a caller:
"I'm not here at the moment."
A logical impossibility,
but also the veiled truth.

When you leave
I am a ghost roaming
without her sensual form,
invisible to herself,
floating away, unmoored,
beyond the heart's racketeering.
I hide my anger
like an obscene tattoo,
but I can punish you
only by disappearing.

THE SAVANT OF SUNFLOWERS,
THE APPRENTICE OF ROSES

Something in a rose
knows to spread its roots
into a stable base,
how to shimmy up a trellis,
graft onto reliable stock,
open rich with scent,
and slowly unfold another
flush of tawny bloom.

While you're away,
I miss the parts of me
that regrow with you:

the mischief elf, the sensual self,
the sonneteering ghost
who rides the flanks of night,
breathing time, sweating stars,
while memories swim
like constellations overhead.

I miss the serpentine Eve
who rarely doses, the attaché
that sometimes imposes,
all the sprites who sprint
through the high supposes,
the patient saint who aspires
to a heaven which encloses,
and, especially, the touched one
committed to the asylum
and penitentiary of roses.

REPORT FROM THE SONNETARIUM

I would not hurt you for the world except
this morning striped roses began to bloom,
it's daylily season, and the garden's adept
at weaving colorful threads without a loom.
Shouldn't I bolt now in summer's hush
when world is fine enough to fill my heart
and worries whisper through the underbrush,
lower key for a while, not off the charts?
Suppose I make a swift preemptive strike
and leave you first, before our circle's run?
An old habit, and not one that I like,
but I can panic down to my skeleton,
and, dismantled, fret in pentameter,
harboring hope, yet failure's amateur.

WHILE YOU'RE AWAY

Five storage boxes clothed
in yellow-and-white plaid fabric
lounge atop my shelves.
They're designed to nest snugly
when empty, a secret throng
the biggest one encapsulates:
a packaged knot, a whole
strengthened by the many's embrace,
a mob of invisible graduates.

Women love things that huddle
neatly inside a belly.
But I've put them all on show,
stacked into Aztec pyramids
on a plateau floating
above the jungle of my wardrobe.
Striped ribbons tie them closed.

Their beauty doesn't lie
in what they contain,
which changes with the season.
Powerful as chant, they cast
bright echoes, festive subtleties
of hue, shape, and feel.

Sometimes I fuss with one
and retie the ribbons—an excuse
to touch harlequin weave,
held fast by silk nails, test the strength
of stiff yet pliant walls,
explore where beauty lies,
as I poke around inside,
wondering how much it will hold,
what shape its space fills,
how loose to risk the ribbons
before the cargo spills.

YOU RETURN

You return
with the fall migration
of hummingbirds.

Perhaps you're driven
by the same restless ongoing
that surges through animal blood
in autumn, a nameless
disquiet in hollow bones
demanding a long solo flight
over oceans to another Eden,
the peninsula of work.

You didn't leave, you say,
just refreshed your sight?
Many animals migrate
by *not* leaving town,
instead burrowing deeper
into fragrant loam,
or choosing a higher den
beyond predator eyes.

I migrate towards us,
a mental niche
beyond complaisance and cold.
I cannot guess the miles.
What is the distance
between the eyes and the soul?

THE SECRET PLACES OF CHILDHOOD

always enfolded me, whether in ice forts
whose milky blue shadows held the world
beyond the walls of sight and size,
or tunneling below dry piles of leaves
matted like cornflakes, or wedged snug
behind mountainous furniture—
say, hiding behind an old pink armchair
spanning a corner, flanked by windows,
removed from the zone of fights,
chores, and related beings,

usually embraced body and soul
through fantasy friends, sweethearts,
parents, colleagues, and animals,
in mind gardens and imaginary jungles
ripe with spy sagas, where desire thrived,
ambition prospered, and nobility
shone through tender heroics,

always existed well beyond words,
in a parallel universe behind the eyes,
which no one shared, or dare discover,
where one planted the small crop
of self, nourishing it with night soil,
somewhere in the wild country of the soul,
returning to Earth heavy and mute
as some swans, whose flyways
evade the time-honored world for a while
and find a refuge, blushing unseen.

WATERCOLOR BY PAUL KLEE

Because your head is a birdcage
    (Jeder Mensch hat seinen Vogel),
because your brows still ladder high in surprise,
because your eye slots accept the large coins of devotion,
because your lips calm a kite wearing a spit curl,
because your sex is a lightpull beneath the hem of an angel
    striding away briskly in pinstripe pants,
because you float above an organ's rosy music
    and flaming exclamation points,
because you don't believe me when I pretend to lie,

dance you monster to my soft song!

Dance You Monster to My Soft Song!, 1922, watercolor and oil transfer drawing on plaster-
grounded gauze mounted on gouache-painted paper

CLOSE AND FAR

close as rain on a leaf
still supple though autumn
colors its cringing
in painfully torrid scarlets
woven thread for thread
beside the genteel greens
of summer when nettles stung
and life's fever zoomed,

far as a plane's flight lofting me
to you, sheathed in metal,
disgorging my soft interior
and rolling overland
to your big bad city of wolves
where I climb through pines
and pinnacles to floor you,

close as married sometimes,
far as the dead bolt
sealing your home's door,
close as the eye of a hurricane
whose torrents thrill the shore
with grief, far as the leash
of a stretching nerve,

close and far, tucked into closets,
aired for silent stroking
along the crease of one's self,
forged by the farrier
sweating blind in my ribs,
that little smithy clanging
molten steel until it bends.

POEMS MAY NOT GEYSER

Poems may not geyser
from the fount of the psyche
every time talking ends.
Chant begins in ribbed caverns
and builds to a simple faith
through a sacrament of song.

No, words may not always spurt
or well from their source,
even if they did until now,
and even though your voice
wraps anger in disappointment
in nonchalance in mission,
all wadded up in sound layers
delicate as mist, even though
your voice steps around
the fraying edges of a sigh.

Oh, I would flay the moment
for the scented bark of songs,
peel the zest from a mood,
even butcher the morning
for you, except that geysers
rarely spring from thirst,
but from earth, in gentle mayhem,
when deep humors churn
and words burst free.

THOSE BITCHES

Quarreling like a pack of hounds,
rowdy selves muscle in,
all shoulder, wagging fast,
leaving no time to muzzle them
or whistle them back.

Lord, can they yammer!
Pedigree and mongrel,
they phase in and out
with canine chutzpah,
barking, leaping,
crouching for your hand.

I've learned it's no use
promising them pools
of sunlight to doze in
or soft toys to nuzzle.

Some days they'd rather
drink from the toilet,
sniff their hinds, romance a leg,
and disembowel baby birds.

Then I cringe, I yowl, I apologize,
I go fetch my stiff-necked pride
and threaten to smother
the watch fires of their eyes.

THOSE ANGELS

Flakes of pure heat, they wing
over the countryside,
blessing all, delivering alms,
haloed in laughter,
peeling the colorful rind of nature,
bathing in starlight.

A river to their people,
they may soak dusty townsfolk
with tingling rains,
or bend an archipelago of words
between neighbors.

They inhabit my village
where they ply the tempting trades
of love and commerce,
and make small sacrifices
on the altar of Surmise.

Visiting often, you let a room
at the inn and hike scenic lanes
between the brambles,
fly-fish in streams where trout
rainbow at the surface,

and dine among angels
who, despite your strict diet
and what will never be, rely on what is
with the dangerous beauty
of a fierce resolve.

I HATE MYSELF TODAY

I hate myself today when we hang up.
Stilted and clumsy, I draped the memory
windows to my steepest fantasies
part funhouse, part mansions of the spirit.

A mind gestapo barred me from crossing
the frontier and climbing those Alps with you.
I stammered, I hedged, I evaded details
like a five-star generalizer.

Was it shame's residue, purity's vengeance,
forgetting my lines on opening night?
Maybe a little urchin bent out of shape?
(Strange how the woman rules the fantasies,
as the child lifts a megaphone of need.)
Though dandy and decent (even in the wilds
of Zanzibar, women lie awake, strumming
their guitars), I felt a fool, humbled by desire.

After our goodbyes, I hate myself
for what I do not show, you do not imply,
the fallen power lines I dare not touch,
all my hang-ups, shortcomings, and alibis.

THE SHELF

Staggering up from the memory mines
after an hour's heavy lifting and eurekas,
I'm shaky from hauling blocks of ragged ore.
Tears form like small tears in a muscle—
an overuse injury from tensing the heart nonstop.
Some say it's those small tears one needs
to build strength—controlled, tempered scars—
but I want to call you and rinse my hot face
with your voice, reach for the last rope
you offered in the darkness, the one I thought
I didn't need, but was wrong about.
Halfway up I rest on the ledge of this poem.

LIGHT AT DAWN

for my father

Beneath a full moon
you lie empty on silk sheets
too fancy for your taste,
your mind blanked
by death's long train whistle,
your cratered heart
beyond apology
and more remote than ever.

I see you alive in flashes
fifty times a day
—face and mannerisms,
hang-ups, obsessions—
a stern go-getter, mighty mite,
and bustling sphinx
whose heart spoke in runes
felt but unutterable,
a man who rang anger
through my ribs
and spoiled me with losses,
yet still stole my love.

After all, after everything,
today I am just a little girl
without her daddy,
flying through a dawn
indistinguishable from sunset,
above the earth and below
a gray coma of clouds.

THE LAMP

The lamp, small sun
shining behind your chair,
spills around your shoulders,
lights delicate hair so softly
you become the child
I never had.

My eyes cross the ottoman,
an empire between us,
and I soothe you, hold you safe
for and against all losses.

Light also hits your glasses
in two brilliant stripes,
as I watch your face flash
into a spectacled cobra
spreading neck ribs wide
like a hooded Pharaoh,
beautiful but venomous,
hissing *fear me, hate me.*

The adorable child again,
then the swaysome cobra,
as my mind pulls from the beat
of our words into artplay
rich with hallucination.

This is how I dilute pain,
that gargoyle drinking,
not by denial but by marvel,
another clever tramp.

It's dark as a wolf's mouth
in these rocky caverns.
But the cleft of insight
is a good place
to hang one's little lamp.

CHRISTMAS

Time again to shut the cupboards
and drape the furniture,
close up the wayfarers' inn
for a spell, cover the clocks,
burn routine, go-as-you-please,
and, if possible, attend
to the clamorings of self.

Pangs fiercely native attack me.
I'm new to this custom of August
and January your tribe keeps.
Surely the days will wander
like an albatross, each wingbeat
a calligraphy for *loss*.

Before parting, we visit
the old city once more,
sway at the wailing wall
in half-light, in hindsight.
I give you another frosted mirror
for your collection—
together they reflect back
to the origin of our universe
and the birth of real time.

In August, I fretted.
How could we pause mid-climb?
Would we remember
our path and purpose?
Would the rope that binds us
loosen, gnaw flesh, slip away?
How would I preserve us?
And yet, at summer's end,
I found you in that pantry
where canned goods, confections,
and memories are stored.

Every heart is a water hole
that must refresh now and then.
Heavy use can muddy it.
I wish you days clear as snowmelt
and other tonics rarely found,
as I place this bookmark
between the pages of thought.

Beginning
to End

...

MISSING

I miss the you I never and cannot have
the way in winter I remember dark ripe cherries
with an ache between hunger and craving,
or miss the banished constellations
in Manhattan, where neon blurs a million stars,
miss you with a sigh light as the breath of starlings,
miss the credenza of those hours
where so many articles of faith were stored,
miss you tremendous and fancy,
the way our minds encompass our work
as it encompasses us, miss you at the edges
of being, the way, when summer dims,
I miss scented air and heat's invisible glove,
miss you the way planets, locked in gravity's embrace,
having everything, a universe in common,
still miss one another as they pass in space,
I miss you missing me, tucked in the wallet
of our past, with eyes big gum balls,
and being beside myself with you newly you.

NOTES FROM THE INTERIOR

On the mind's quiet battlefield,
where impulses duel,
the flesh tent of my body
echoes with your voice
and your face hovers before me
like a wartime melody.

Lengthy, with huge hands,
you look down upon me
as only gods and parents do.
There are no bedtime stories.
Your life is a closed book.
And yet, it's by reading you
reading me trying to read you
I build idioms of acceptance
from grief's residue.

Real as rain, you also exist
as pure icon in deep space,
where the sun loiters at noon,
the cozy physics we rely on fails,
and I need to reach a hand back
as I sit, in case the chair fled
when I wasn't looking.

In that wonderland
of small things, an offhand remark
looms large as the Orient,
a simple word can strike hot
as ball lightning, an idle gesture
crush the delicate threads
of hope's tapestry.

There I long for the impossible
heaven we all desire,
where we belong to someone,
good friends, and everyone,
welcome in a world
where hearts are never broken,
our coming and going pleases,
and needs, however selfish,
are met as soon as spoken.

Although we meet head to head,
our lives don't really mesh,
and I doubt you need me
with the same vertigo,
which both alarms and disarms me.
But I sense you take to heart
my wilderness, where I risk
the awkward, tense, visceral need
to know what feels most real
before the letting go.

IMAGINING THE DIVINE

On cold days, the divine haunts
the exhalations of squirrels
whose breath hovers
starch-white as tiny souls.

Like the sky, heaven begins
at one's feet. Look down.
The red-winged blackbird's rasp
sounds angelic, summer croons
pontifications of light,
and, my god, life fancies trees.

Because I believe we become
a neverthriving of dreams,
all our senses leveled,
I imagine the divine
drawing on of evening,
belted at the waist,
the divine cloud-slung stars
burning black holes
into the fabric of night,

I divine the lusty sun
in each aching-green leaf,
and revere the silver
ceremonies of the moon
cradled in its own arms.

Just imagine the divine
hilltops padded with trees,
the bone-wings of a river basin
hipped in daylilies, Canada goose chicks:
fluff-budgets that waddle.

Before my one and only
three-pound universe, I stand
in judgment, alone with the world,
so long as we both shall live,
or vanish when eyelids close.

Because life will have been all
my days, I imagine the divine
face of my loving dear,
who shares the harsh and softer fate-falls
inside these garden walls
where the divine agency of love
will have mattered in the end
more than faith, call, reward,
or a vein of panting stars.

Like the planet, we seemed
to be traveling through space
but were always in a holding pattern
between the earth and sky,
waiting to unbecome, plural once more.

THE ANT LION'S DREAM

Hearing through a megaphone of touch,
I choose a crater and listen for faint
signs of tumbling. The world skids
into my sand funnel. Disturb
the tiniest grain and I feel it,
move a dust mote and I
stiffen, fangs quivering.
I am just one way the
earth cups its hands.
Drop in anytime.

UNCERTAINTY PRINCIPLE

That hot and cold extremes
may rub without blurring
strikes me like a gunshot
I do not report to you
because I'm steadying words
on long columns of air
in the ancient amphitheater
of my distress, where gladiators
wrestle with lions of loss.

My lips are shaping words
realer than the fears
they assemble (a sorry lot),
minting coins of my realm
to fill your ears with gold
sometimes, today with baser metals
bearing my likeness.

This nickel-plated worry
about a good choice I made
in slow anger, and have been whittling
and writhing about ever since,
I confide in shame, turning
fraying pockets inside out,
wishing I could put all my strife
and muddle in your hands,
agent-parent-knight-protector.

Outside, snowflakes big as bees
lure me to open country
and long white paragraphs
where, later, fastening on skis,
I crouch behind your shield
and unfasten my thoughts
while birds whirl overhead

like crib toys, and tranquillity
is a hundred mad instincts
and motions holding each other
still between glides.

MATINS

as a wild dark iridescent bird
loves the wilderness it patrols
over ice-festooned hamlets
with feathers and hollow bones
somehow held rigid enough
to carve invisible steel
and steer a steady arc
through nor'easter, wind shear or fog,
gauging the prickly space
before and aft, at times riding
the smooth air leaders dole out,
and at others rising up the ranks
to break a fresh trail
through miles of perfumed
yet unendurable sky,
reading sun path, star maps,
and muscular terrain,
while perfecting the knack
of wedging with strangers;

as light loves quartz,
with a mineral love that chants
from the bones outward,
beyond wilt or sense
as a child loves the rustling
of stiff coats,
or a woman loves slumbering
loose as rumpled silk
in full view
behind half-opened eyes.

NOT IN THE NOW SO MUCH

The shipwreck looks hazy—
a veil away
as in a fading photograph.
People still die in my arms,
but at oar's length,
not in the now so much,
though sad and grim
with horror stuck
like napalm's clinging fire.
Ever since, I've drowned
in that coral shambles.
But today the jaws of time
feel slacker, the film grainier.
Someone oiled the lens.
I still recall the waves of death,
the kiss and touch, but far away,
not in the now so much.

LAST WEEK

Which door
you slammed
in my face
I have forgotten,
but not the splinters
raking my mouth,
or varnish
dark and sweet
as violin resin.

Using words
like "wrong" and "mistake,"
you exiled me
beyond our new
found land,
to a wilderness
of dusty magic
and voluminous need.

My shame is all
firecrackers:
a long string
of burning noise.

Legless as thought,
I am a scramble
of leavings, as I run
from the garden
where you moved
between plaster gods.
I left my heart
like a hand grenade
among the statues.

BENEATH THE SHEETS

Though you know the unknown and unknowing
severals of me, and I know your hands
hold the delicate white vellum, sails of skin,
carried to you by the page of the poem,
and how lately I miss those facsimile selves
both lofty and sensuous, spanning the miles,
I send you this anyway to enter and re-enter
as the spirit moves you, because in this moment
I trust that felt can be said, trust your passion,
our union, your calling, in this moment,
stilled by words stark as blood drops on snow,
white-hot as a molten poem taking shape
in your hands now like an amulet of desire.

NO'S KNIFE AT YES'S THROAT

Two cycling accidents:
a collision with a car
at a busy intersection,
a curb-rub and topple
while biking around a lake.

The first left a contusion
the shape of China on my thigh,
a purple archipelago
down one leg, and left shoulder
jammed into its socket.
I felt lucky to limp away,
bruised but intact.

The second fall a week later
gashed my arm on gravel
and wrenched my right shoulder
where pain still bleats
louder than codeine quiets.
I'll learn today if it's broken,
can heal, how and when;
the sling will make writing,
biking, gardening a trial.

Two nightmares in a row:
the first falls in a dozen years.
Coincidence, friends say.
Maybe it's body talk, a *non serviam*
hissed by bone and muscle.
You urged me to roam again,
but I can't, you see. Sidelined
by injury. My flesh is rent.

Dad's death, mom's cancer,
crack-up with my last therapist,
Aunt Fatima's death,
changing publisher and agent
(familiars for a decade),
carpal tunnel, Paul's illnesses,
sweet hours of writing sweat
(but under the gun), plus the usual
crazy fret and bother of a life,
tire blowout to gas leak—
I can't shoulder another ounce.
My pockets sag with cargo
as I wade deeper and deeper
in the shoals of endurance.

You meant well, dear man,
yet I partly blame you for this pain
my body may have chosen
rather than disappoint you,
or, worse, smudge an image
of me sparkling in your brain,
chosen touchable wounds
as the lesser risk and strain.

YOU PHONE UNEXPECTEDLY
WHILE I'M WRITING

Suddenly you.
Your voice limns your face
one piece at a time:
a fast jigsaw puzzle.

I hurry towards you
from great distance
        (You hear me saying hello)
across a mind bridge
where word images leap like goats
among crags of memory
        (You hear me confirming
        a change of date),

where language isn't spoken
but seen, and the landscape lives
only if stared at, diamond hard
        (You hear me chatting
        about upcoming holidays).

I haven't time to prepare
a face to meet you,
or get the kids dressed up
        (You tell me your phone's
        still out, you're on your cell phone).

Such a luxury, this:
when I'm between worlds
I see how you see me seeing you:
off-duty, less intimate,
caring as much and not differently,
yet holding a pyramid in place
        (You hear me laughing, saying goodbye).

DREAM CYCLE

Never was wind so physical
a dream: all punch and swoon
with cold roaring up the nostrils,
and rawhide cutting the neck
in whipcracks. The sound:
wet sheets flapping on a line.

At a stoplight, when we pause,
the wind grows stern
in its absence: cheeks flush,
hands ache in hot drams of stillness.

The motorcycle lurches into gear,
another absence, the clutch jars,
jars again, and sends us zooming
on a blade through ice tunnels.

Dipping low around a turn,
pillow-close to gravel,
the engine's heavy panting
revs my pulse as we pivot
on iron air and become pure
speed and weight: streaming metal:
swinging up through balance
and counterbalance, climbing
a steep arpeggio of gears,
until noise hits a deafening calm
that blurs everything but us.
At 60 m.p.h., the motorcycle hangs
motionless, grazing on blacktop.
Sunlight glazes the winter-bashed wheat.
The highway pours like lava.

Then the bike staggers in slow-motion
and whips around a turn, surging
past fields, gardens, people,
and somewhere between gears
the frantic world hardens
for one level moment into sense.

LIKE YOUR FACE,
A THOUSAND-LEAFED DAY

after Hans Magnus Enzensberger

Like your face,
a thousand-leafed day,
and I who rejoice
in what's measureless
measure the onset of evening
and the imagined scent
of your eyelashes
shivering like flowers in the wind.

What fate threw us together?
The same chance
that drew air lanes for the bats
swooping like neuroses
from the sky, fluttering
over frail autumn leaves
which cannot harm or save
or be anyone's victim.

ONE MORNING

we talk between the fence men
and the heavy machinery
I must keep a close eye on
and pleasantries with the nursing student
who runs errands for me
and the woman in the telephone company
start-up department in Richmond
and the trash collection start-up
department in Richmond
and the Computer Help desk lady
in Richmond and searching the Internet
for painted botanical tiles
I must find and approve
before leaving the house
to reconstructive strangers
and e-mailing my agent
with thirty possible titles
none of which is quite right
for my unnameable new book
and answering a call from a friend
who is worried and frustrated
and angry altogether
because her mother refuses
to take her painkillers and antidepressants
and when my friend asks how I'm doing
sharing my less dire emergency
of being in absolute title hell
and afterwards e-mailing congratulations
to my goddaughter at Boston U.
who has just finished her training
as a telephone crisis counselor
and e-mailing the construction lady
with whom I share my Internet find
and grabbing a mouthful of chili
I eat too fast to enjoy

and then closing my lavender door
on the world and retreating
to where I always sit when we talk
in that alcove your ghost inhabits
so clearly and after dialing your number
and we exchange good mornings
I fight you for my guilt
which after all is one of my few possessions
but soon I'm wading into the deep
persona I floated above all morning
and making you work hard
to find me where it's tempting to hide
beneath the fine rubble
that passes for everyday life.

BEGINNING TO END

As this book rounds off,
I start grieving. How I love
tying the shoelaces of poems
on workday mornings,
schooling them for hours,
knowing the last train of thought
you could receive before Monday
has to depart by Thursday at 5:50 P.M.

A tight timetable, but that regime
helps focus my urgent need
to stanch heartflow, dam the bleed
behind the linen tourniquets
of words. *Velum, vellum.*
I sometimes get them confused.
Which one do I scribble on?
Which one suture and soothe?

I love using the poems as clues,
telegrams, and invisible ink
you decipher better than I do.
Some solder us together
with the molten lead of ambiguity.
In others I wrestle demons
or anger openly without shame.
Through candor and chaos
they witness the grief and embargo
of our work, bountiful, yet finite.

Now I no longer require
these walking sticks to grip
as I mountaineer with you,
and it was hard carving,
but I loved the damp wood
in my hands, hearing the blade glide,
smelling the sticky varnish.

I loved how the poems served
as pegs, flagstaffs, banisters,
telegraph poles, crutches,
shafts, hitching posts, or tongues,
depending on our whereabouts,
whim, or flagrant need.

Hollow, craving song, I long
to find my feet again, and rendezvous
in verse, but I feel blessed
by our fine entanglement
that somehow seals the past
and allows a chance to renew—
and grateful too for these wildflowers
gathered in sun and rain
along the lowlands with you.

WHO'S THERE?

I don't understand my muse either.
Oh, sure—the yes and no of him,
the familiar echo of his feet on paper,
his voice in the exuberant trill
of house wrens, the he/she/it gender-blur
who's mainly a him (because he fills
my hollows and limbs), the toss and turn
of him under the sheets, and the way he seeps
into your face through eyes and mouth
(I'm surprised you don't feel him
bustling around your bone house).

But he doesn't show me his calendar
where red-letter days and vacations
are circled, and just when I think
he's cursed me and fled, he reappears
drunk and demands to be fed.

So, I think he has finished this book,
but I may be wrong. He knows better than I
the lyrics to the songs we must sing
due to his sensibility and my need.
Hands trembling, I type what's painful to admit:
"This is the last poem in my book."

Then ghostly keys move, and *he* types: "It isn't."

ALL FIRES THE FIRE

As snow falls today, I marvel
how differently we ply our trades,
and yet they both transport us
like sleigh horses, not beasts of burden,
over ice fields, across ditches,
through chancy woods.
We rely on their unique gait and speed,
dress them in bells and fineries,
hide their lather, mask our galloping need.

That reminds me of Genghis Khan
who bested worlds on blunt,
shaggy little ponies, which grazed
winter wheat from the vanquished fields
and slaughtered well if blizzards raged
or edibles failed. When all the newborns
were eaten, he'd milk the mares
to curdle yogurt and cheese,
then brew the alcoholic *kumiss,*
eating the mares only as last resort.

Centuries later, Rommel fought
his desert wars the same as Khan,
strike and withdraw, strike and withdraw,
and would have won the world
with a tank were it not for lack of oil
leaving him stranded in sand.
For all his savvy, he missed the truth
Khan's belly understood: in the last
of last days, even essentials grow
awkward fast, and you can afford to lose
almost everything: love, money,
shelter, warmth, renown: everything
but the shaggy beast that sustains you.

GRACE

I

White carnations
slouch
in a green glass vase
before the picture window,

as pink tremolos
of sunset,
whole sentences of light,
drift through
the Venetian blinds.

The sun keens itself
in a curve
of the vase,
fizzing yellow.

II

On the lawn of memory,
    violets suddenly appear: each a sensation

like a note, but without the dirge of loss,
    translucent, welcome, unexpected.

Photo albums open their leaves
    with a calm that seems phenomenal.

Tonight the sun reclines in the sky,
    and time is a kneeling animal.

THE WAY OF OUR KIND

Borrowed heart, constant
among fleeting forms,
you're an amalgam of desires
like me, a man whose history
I dare not know, but assume
to be riddled by fate's gifts
and treacheries—happenstance
being the way of our kind.

No doubt your life unfolds
like mine: intense, unplanned,
stoic at times, badly judged
now and then, now and then
right as a summer sky,
and blessed by small acts
of mercy and heroism—rescue
being the way of our kind.

I'm curious about deep self:
your dreams and stratagems,
how your mind fidgets,
what makes your heart quiver,
the fictions that brace you
and truths on which you rely—
curious not simply as a wish
for more, but because kinship
is the way of our kind.

Because it is the way
of our kind, you and I,
we ladle ideas like hot steel,
deliberate and tense,
growing amazed at times
by scalding beauty
in the forge of the mind

that can burn or build cities
and love in pantomime.

How lucky we are
to share this planet and climb.
I would have said that
earlier, without obliquity
and rhyme, but felt shy—
because fondness equals surrender,
and a camouflaged heart
is the way of our kind.

Still, I won't always see you
sitting across from me,
your cheekbones perishable
as thread, as summer,
or hear your voice pouring
into my ear like dye,
but I will miss the little
I know of you, manner and mind,
because caring and missing
is the way of our kind.

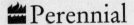 Perennial

Books by Diane Ackerman:

ORIGAMI BRIDGES
Poems of Psychoanalysis and Fire
ISBN 0-06-055529-7 (paperback)

At the heart of *Origami Bridges* is the delicate relationship of trust between analyst and patient, a relationship that grows out of the emotional give-and-take of the psychoanalytic process. In this collection, Diane Ackerman lays bare her desires, anger, jealousy, fears, and anxiety as she probes not only her present emotional landscape but also her past. What gradually rises to the surface is an understanding of how Ackerman uses verse to purge her demons, express her delight, or confess secret longing, and through this process come to a better understanding of the self.

"Witty and honest. . . . [*Origami Bridges*] is a resounding success."
—*Library Journal*

CULTIVATING DELIGHT
A Natural History of My Garden
ISBN 0-06-050536-2 (paperback)

Written in sensuous, lyrical prose, *Cultivating Delight* celebrates the sensory pleasures and unique insights offered by gardens and the seasons. Whether deadheading flowers or glorying in the profusion of roses, offering sugarwater to a hummingbird or studying the slug, Ackerman welcomes the unexpected drama and extravagance as well as the sanctuary it offers. Ackerman's garden nourishes its creator, who imaginatively returns the favor and seizes privileged moments to leap from science and metaphor to meditation on the human condition.

"Ackerman's book reminds us that we, too, can make our paradise here and that tranquility can be achieved by contemplating the petals of a rose."
—*New York Times Book Review*

ALSO BY
DIANE ACKERMAN

Cultivating Delight
Deep Play
I Praise My Destroyer
A Slender Thread
The Rarest of the Rare
A Natural History of Love
A Natural History of the Senses
The Moon by Whale Light
Jaguar of Sweet Laughter
Reverse Thunder
On Extended Wings
Lady Faustus
Twilight of the Tenderfoot
Wife of Light
The Planets: A Cosmic Pastoral

FOR CHILDREN

Monk Seal Hideaway
Bats: Shadows in the Night

ANTHOLOGY

The Book of Love

Toshi Otsuki, courtesy of *Victoria magazine*

About the Author

Poet, essayist, and naturalist, DIANE ACKERMAN was born in
Waukegan, Illinois. *Cultivating Delight: A Natural History of
My Garden* is her most recent book. She is also the author of
many highly acclaimed works of nonfiction, including the
bestselling *A Natural History of the Senses*.

Her poetry has appeared in literary journals and magazines,
and has been collected into several volumes, including *Jaguar
of Sweet Laughter: New and Selected Poems* and *I Praise My Destroyer*.

Diane Ackerman has received many prizes and awards,
among them the John Burroughs Nature Award and the Lavan
Poetry Prize. She has taught at several universities, including
Columbia, New York University, and Cornell, where she is
visiting professor at the Society for the Humanities. Diane
Ackerman lives in upstate New York.